DAISY CHAINS

PLANTS OF CHILDHOOD

CHRIS HOWKINS

PUBLISHED BY
CHRIS HOWKINS

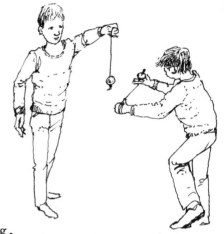

COVER PHOTOGRAPH - Ox-eye Daisies
                  photo Chris Howkins (c)

CONTENTS

PREFACE

We all know where babies come from. Mums and dads find them under the Gooseberry bushes! That's the story for curious young enquirers of this century, although nobody seems to know from where the idea came. The earliest written record is only from 1944 although older readers will remember it in use long before that. Having emerged from under our spiny 'birthplaces' we have all gone on to have a childhood. As with all aspects of life it has been connected closely with plants, although at first we might not think so.

This volume introduces some of the range of those connections, both past and present, through the themes of child rearing, good behaviour, rituals, counting, toys, games, work and herbal medicine. Many readers will be surprised that childhood as we think of it dates only from the first years of this century and that previously there was a quick transition from babyhood to young adult (see the Introduction). That in many ways has restricted the material available to use in a study such as this but nevertheless the aim has not been to try and include 'all' the material but to select out interesting representatives.

St. Marks
School
Godalming.

INTRODUCTION

Childhood is a modern luxury. For thousands of years there was no such thing, as we know it, just a rapid transfer from the dependency of babyhood directly to becoming a young adult. This did not change until the early years of this century, primarily with the passing of the 'Children's Charter' of 1908. Therefore, to study the plants that have been associated with youngsters is a far more limited theme than might be imagined but nevertheless has some charming, fascinating and intriguing associations. Some are thousands of years old while others must be new - like children in a school garden in 1994 who were heard to call the Bindweed 'Maggie Thatcher Weed'.

Until the rise of a middle class of merchants and industrialists etc. there were just the two broad groups of the workers and their superiors. For the workers there was that direct transition out of babyhood into being a productive member of the family. This solved the problem of child-minding, even when older girls could act as mum's deputy, when the mother had to work. It also absorbed the youngster into imitating their elders and could earn an essential extra penny or two for the household. Today we view 'child labour' with suspicion to say the least but for thousands of years it has been normal practice and for the last two thousand years ordained by God from the Bible text, "He that doth not work neither shall he eat."

Thus the lace-makers, for example, initiated both boys and girls into the lace 'schools' at about five years of age. In such ways working infants earned a few pennies that could be vital for their family's survival and at the same time they began their training for later life. Even seemingly mundane jobs, like bird-scaring in the fields, were turned to advantage. The children went armed with slings and learned to be expert shots, like David in the Bible, and they killed the birds: "Four and twenty blackbirds baked in a pie" is not just a nursery rhyme but an image drawn from everyday life. Blackbirds fetched 2d a dozen in the late medieval markets.

Today childhood.
(for the rich!)

Childhood did not last much longer in the noble households either, for as soon as children grew out of their baby clothes they were dressed in small versions of adult costumes and trained to match their social skills. When still only a few years old they were likely to be moved to another noble household to continue their training in a more independent setting. It was not easy to belong to two families when those families took opposing sides in the interminable conflicts.

In later times the boys of wealthier households were packed off to new boarding schools and to preparatory schools and this did create a stage more akin to what we would call childhood.

School Art Class
on the tow-path
Murray's Bridge.
1981

Schools were also developing for the middle class
that evolved out of medieval trade. By the close of
the 14th century there were about 400 grammar schools
in England and by 1406 parliament had made statutory
that "every man or woman, of what state or condition he
be, shall be free to take their son or daughter to take
learning at any school that pleaseth them, within the
realm." It would still take hundreds of years to make
that a reality.

Although the early institutions worked long hours
there were, nevertheless, periods of spare time and
energy to be contained, particularly in the boarding
schools. Here was scope for 'childhood' activities,
such as organised games that involved as many pupils
as possible with the fewest staff. Thus a statement
from Guildford in 1598 records, that forty years
earlier the land at the junction of the High Street
and North Street was where the boys of the Free
School (today's Royal Grammar School) "did runne and
play there at cricket." This is claimed to be the
earliest record of cricket. However, its origins are
obscure there are earlier references to something
similar at least. Edward I as a youngster played at
'creagit' - from a Saxon word for stick (bat).

7

Schooling was a luxury as only a few families could afford non productive members. Nevertheless education gradually came to be seen as valuable and so to change attitudes schooling was described as a type of work. Thus arose the concepts of schoolwork and homework, of working hard at school and working for exams and so forth, that are still with us today.

Even in the early 1900s a quarter of school children, aged 5-12, had paid employment. By this time child labour was not just vital to the household economy but to the national economy as well. Only young children were small enough to work the narrow seams down the mines or small enough to crawl under the machines in the northern textile mills. Industrialists opposed education for fear it was a threat to their wealth and productivity. They argued that to educate the poor was a pointless and thankless expense that would lead only to insurrection. Trouble was already at hand though. It was the factory children running amok in Gloucester on Sundays that inspired Robert Raikes to found the Sunday schools movement. Thus the 19th century Education Acts are in the plural as the concept had to be introduced in stages and with caution so that even the Act for compulsory education for all children had limitations compared with today's expectations and legislation.

Families still needed their children to contribute to the family income and it was legal for children to have part-time paid employment during school hours. There were two ways of working this in the factory system, either working half days or alternate days. In the countryside work was more likely to be seasonal, primarily at the times of various harvest such as for apples, hops, potatoes etc. School holidays came to be timed accordingly and the summer holiday was recorded regularly as the harvest holiday. School attendance records show girls absent on Mondays and Fridays, the prime days for laundering and cleaning respectively. This was their preparation for domestic service. How amazed they would have been to learn that soon children would be paid to do nothing but pocket money and parental allowances were still to come.

HOP PICKING - one of the seasonal harvests at which
the children were employed but which
was not specific to them.

The usual age for leaving school, by the turn of the century was 12- 13 which was legally permissible if the child passed the Labour Exam or else had clocked up 300 school attendances in the previous five years. This was not abolished until after the First World War.

The 20th century brought in new changes that created an extended notion of childhood and introduced many of the ideas we hold today. Those who had been thought of as young adults were reclassified - no longer could they gamble, smoke or drink under the age of fourteen. This became the new age for leaving school and part-time working/schooling was phased out. There were new ideas on the age for criminal responsibility and so forth.   (See Steve Humphries in References)

It is against this background that 'the plants of childhood' have been sought. For many children, if not most, the associations would have been in a working capacity. These have, on the whole, been omitted from this study as they are part of the story of particular occupations. Plants were also important in many of the special celebrations, such as May Day, but these were originally celebrated by the whole community, even if ultimately they became child-orientated, such as 5th November for Bonfire Night. One representative, Shik-shak Day has been included. Many of these died out through the times of increased industrialism or became such a relief that they degenerated into rowdiness and were banned, such as St.Catherine's Fair at Guildford. Even in such remote places as Shetland's Lerwick the Viking festival of Up-Helly-Aa was banned in 1874 for being too rowdy. In 1889 the procession was revived. Many other events came in for revival too, especially in these modern times of nostalgia, such as the Black Cherry Fair at Chertsey, Surrey. They are still family occasions but for families of an age of nylon and plastic, factory produce and supermarkets, far removed from the days when plants had to be employed directly to serve the everyday needs of our ancestors.

RUSH PLAITING
for making the
rush bonnets;
one of several
cottage crafts
centred upon
plants.

SPELLINGS, SOURCES AND
ACKNOWLEGEMENTS

The information has as usual been culled from files
compiled over twenty five years, and so thanks are due
to all the correspondents who have been contributors.
More specifically, thanks are due to : Mavis Budd,
Ruth Hardy, Roy Vickery, Gordon Weaver and Ruth Wyllie
for their assistance in the final checking of some
material ready for publication. Thanks also to the
Surrey Primary Schools at Worplesdon and St.Mark's at
Godalming, for the opportunities to work with their
children and use the illustrations. Printed sources
quoted in the text are listed in the References at the
end.

Of the organisations that have been of great help in
the final preparation particular thanks are due to the
Dictionary Department of Oxford University Press which
was not only as willing as ever to answer enquiries
but went to great lengths to help with the correct
usage of the -ary and -ery endings to confectionery.
Even they found that complicated but decided which to
use after the text was read to them! In common with
some other writers the references to fairies have been
given the old spelling of faeries, from before the
Victorians tamed them for children's fairy tale books.
Similarly, the old practice of spelling English plant
names with a capital initial has been retained to save
confusion over adjectives.

Additional assistance of
particular note was given
by British Sugar plc,
Food From Britain,
Museum of London,
The Rocking Horse
Workshop at Wem,
Shropshire, and the
Weybridge Information
Centre of Surrey
County Library.

"Better to have one plough working
than two cradles rocking."
Proverb

CRADLE DAYS

"Fair in the cradle,
foul in the saddle."
Proverb

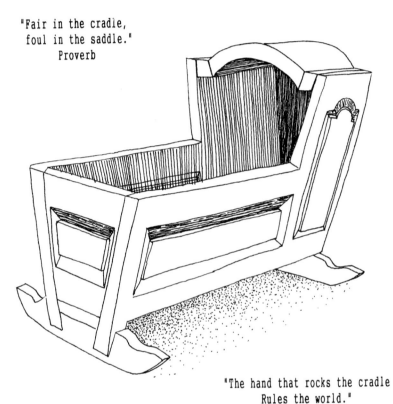

"The hand that rocks the cradle
Rules the world."
Proverb

Cradle Land - that to be inherited
by the youngest heir or be shared
rather than inherited by eldest heir.

Cradle drawings courtesy of Anthony Welling,
17th and 18th Century Oak Furniture,
Ripley, Surrey.

CRADLE DAYS

Cradles or creddles are very ancient; the name comes from the language of the Saxons but they were known before that. The Saxons slept on the floor around the central hearth, or, on benches, so any special provision for babies is all the more impressive. Those early cradles were probably of woven wicker work, especially if the word does have a connection with those woven baskets known as creels, which is uncertain. Perhaps they were suspended from a roof beam, not just for ease of rocking but to lift the baby clear of the draughts, rats and mice that would all have invaded a Saxon home. Such cradles could have been unhooked and carried like a modern carry-cot; certainly medieval manuscript illuminations show carrying devices, as illustrated. They appear to be of woven linen canvas, or leather, stretched over a wooden frame, probably of Hazel or perhaps Ash.

There are several tantalising references to the probability that in Britain and abroad it was once normal to hang cradles from branches of trees, out of doors to rock in the wind. Hence the popular lullaby:

Rock-a-bye baby on the tree top,
When the wind blows the cradle will rock.
When the bough breaks the cradle will fall.
Down will come baby, cradle and all.

The words are so old that their origins cannot be traced although linguistically the surviving versions indicate a Saxon origin.

However, some think the idea goes back to Ancient Egypt and the baby was the god Horus whereas others claim it was "the first poem produced on American soil" from the belief that it is the work of a colonist off the Mayflower who was impressed with native American hanging cradles made of Birch bark.

14

Late medieval baby carrier (twins).

Late medieval cradle with detachable rockers.

"THE FOOT AT THE CRADLE, AND THE HAND AT THE ROKE IS THE SIGN OF A GOOD HOUSEWIFE"

People have also struggled to find a meaning to the rhyme. Some think it is to do with tragedy, in the theatrical sense, whereby the hero rises to high status and falls through no direct fault of his own. In some versions the tree is specified as a Holly and yet the Holly rarely grows spreading boughs suitable for supporting such a cradle but it does make sense if it were symbolic, devolved from one of the early church dramas when Holly was used as a symbol of Christ.

Woven cradles were made from species of Willow and there are still craftsmen making them today, exploiting the range of 'basket willows' still grown for such weaving. In the days before any accurate classification of these very confusing trees they were generally put into one of two groups: the shrubby species, known as Sallows, and the tree species, known as Osiers. The latter were preferred for cradles, according to John Evelyn. He noted also that the long pliant suckers from Lime trees were used and no doubt he could have mentioned others that were used for weaving, such as the Spindle (Euonuymus europaeus) and the Dogwood (Cornus sanguinea). They were not grown in specific plantations like the 'basket willows' but were culled when and where available, being known as 'hedge basket' materials.

When cradles came to be made of solid wood they could be too heavy or cumbersome for overhead suspension. Instead they were provided with rockers, which were sometimes detachable. They extended into foot-pieces so that the mother's hands were free for work. Thus in 1721 James Kelly, explaining Scottish ways to the English reported that "The Foot at the Cradle, and the Hand at the Roke [distaff] is the Sign of a good House-Wife."

A second design was without rockers and became known by the mid 17th century as a crib. The simple chest style persisted for centuries, with the addition of corner finials as hand-holds for rocking and finally hoods were added. By the 18th century they had reached their finest form, after which fabric hoods were used.

Any timber could be used, with Oak being preferred, as it was for most domestic items, but there was one great exception and that was the Elder which was most definitely taboo. Elder is the tree most associated with evil in the folklore of North West Europe and to use the wood in the construction of a cradle would be irresponsible. It would attract the Devil down the chimney into the cradle to sleep on the baby's face and suffocate it, or, the Devil would pinch the baby black and blue all over. These are not beliefs to sneer at but attempts to explain cot deaths and blueness after asphyxiation. In some districts they feared the Devil would steal the baby while in others they blamed his visit for the baby sickening and dying. Mental problems were explained in later life as resulting from having had "a knock in the cradle."

To gain protection from such demons parents tried placing a short piece of Rowan (Sorbus aucuparia) under the bottom blanket. Where the cradle had detachable rockers then these should have been made of Rowan. The tree was regarded as all powerful especially by the Celtic peoples and many of the beliefs associated with it are still known, if not practised, today. That is so, not just in Celtic Wales, Ireland and Scotland but right down in S.E.England.

In England and France, however, the all powerful tree has been the Hawthorn and so that is what must be put in cradles in these countries. Presumably the thorns were expected to deter the Devil.

ROWAN spring growth

17

CRADLE HERBS

"The cradle straws are scarce out of his breeches," runs an English proverb, making it clear how commonly straw was used for padding for the cradles. Into the straw, or hay, various herbs were strewn which came to be known as 'cradle herbs'.

Presumably these once included plants believed to ward off evil but which the Christian missionaries suppressed. Nevertheless, there was still a need for deodorant herbs and these were duly given Christian myths to sanctify their continued use. The myths were founded on the belief that herbs were added to the hay in the manger at the Nativity. Of course in the days of mixed pastures there would indeed have been many wild flowers among the grasses cut and dried for hay. No specific reference to their presence survives in Bible texts but then that is also true of the animals in the stable, yet they are present in Nativity illustrations from the earliest times. This is used to argue that the Bible is not the immutable Word of God but has been edited and that at some early date it was considered unseemly for the Son of God to be born among animals. Maybe the herbs went too - if they were ever there.

Three herbs in particular have reputations for being the 'true' cradle herbs of the Nativity but they create a rather tangled history. Of central importance is the ever popular Thyme of garden and kitchen.
By 1527 it was known in print as 'Unser Frawen Betstro' which was translated literally into English by Henry Lyte in 1578 as Our Lady's Bedstraw. For some reason he changed the plant so that Our Lady's Bedstraw was no longer Thyme but the plant known today as Lady's Bedstraw. The 'Our' was soon dropped in Protestant England.

With the change came new myths and so we hear that at the birth of Christ there were two herbs in the manger hay, of which only one rose up in adoration at the holy birth. God blessed that one and changed its flowers from white to gold and this is England's Lady's Bedstraw. The second herb was cursed by God for not responding and forbidden to flower ever again. This was the Bracken fern.

Nativity scene, c.1500,
sketched from the only
church brass of such;
Cobham, Surrey.
Note the smallest Shepherd
bears an iron shod wooden
spade.

Lady's Bedstraw has been one of the most popular of strewing herbs for cradles and elsewhere because it contains a lot of coumarin, the compound which gives the sweet smell to hay. The more the plant dries the stronger the scent becomes, especially when warmed. Its relative, Sweet Woodruff (Galium odoratum) tends to work even better but is of coarser growth. Neither would be toxic to the baby.

Now for the third of those herbs. It was a species of mint called Pennyroyal (Mentha pulegium) which was formerly far better known than it is today. Unlike its relatives, this is a little low creepy mint that can be quite tricky to grow, but, if it likes your garden will smother it before you've finished your tea-break. The name has nothing to do with coinage but comes from the French for non other than the Thyme! This derivation has given rise to much debate.

Looking at the botanical name, the specific 'pulegium' derives ultimately from the Latin 'pulex' for flea, as this plant is an effective repellent and we can see why it was used in cradles. The American Pennyroyal, incidently, is a different plant, Hedeoma pulegiodes, which has similar properties and blends of the two herbs have been used medicinally.

Lady's
Bedstraw

20

Thus the association between Thyme and babies has been long, varied and valid. Those wonderful aromatic oils in the herb contain thymol which is powerfully antiseptic, antibacterial and antifungal. It is so effective that it is still in great use today, in our deodorants, mouthwashes, gargles and other toiletries. Being so powerful it needs using with respect. The old advice that the herb should be rubbed on to the gums of teething babies should be ignored as the oils can act as a powerful irritant.

It would have helped keep the bedstraw sweet and was said to keep flies away. That was tested recently and Thyme was indeed found to be repellent to house flies. It was also said to stop bed-wetting (enuresis) and that too was tested with a report in 1972 of a success rate of 85% in six weeks. Similarly, it can be used against children's diarrhoea.

It promotes a good sleep too and for that reason the old claims of it warding off nightmares were to some extent valid. As for the belief that it would enable children to see the faeries... well... maybe! When we read that Thyme blooms were laid upon the eyelids of children to let them see the faeries it sounds like an excellent ruse to persuade sleepless children to lie still and quiet with their eyes closed! It was also said that the most potent Thyme of all had to be taken from off a faerie throne and that does sound rather risky! Certainly this association with the little folk caused the plant to be banished from many a household whatever its virtues and people still refuse to have it indoors as I discovered when I took a pot of Thyme to a talk in Berkshire. (Parsley is another herb I have learned not to take to talks!)

CAT-TAIL COMFORT

For wonderful soft down to provide warmth and comfort in cradles, nappies and on cradle boards there was little to compare with that provided by the waterside plant here illustrated.

When the big brown seed heads ripen they break up to let the seeds float off on silky parachutes. Just before this moment the heads can be harvested and the down stripped off. Gerard recorded it being gathered around Ely and the Fens for sale to stuff mattresses for ploughmen and the poor but records of it are scant. That's because most recorders were middle class for whom it was not fitting to enquire too deeply into the ways of the poor (they themselves used the much more expensive duck down) but when enquiring minds went to the New World it was quite acceptable to record the ways of the native Americans. Thus we learn that such peoples as the Chippewa, Flambeau Ojibwe, Huron, Meskwaki and Potawatomi of the United States and Canada all used this native plant in various ways.

It has its drawbacks. The Flambeau Ojibwe people had to boil theirs first to get rid of bugs while in Sweden they gave up using it because it goes lumpy once slept on, unless vigorously shaken each day. Nevertheless, it has been used widely in sleeping bags, mattresses, quilts and cradles and also as a nappy lining where it helped keep the baby clean too.

As for its name, well that's a tangled tale. By the time the colonists went over to America it was known as Cats-tail and has remained so. In Britain, however, it became Greater Reedmace (Typha latifolia) until people began calling it 'bullrush', especially since the artist Sir Lawrence Alma-Tadema painted his 'Moses in the Bullrushes' in Greater Reedmace.

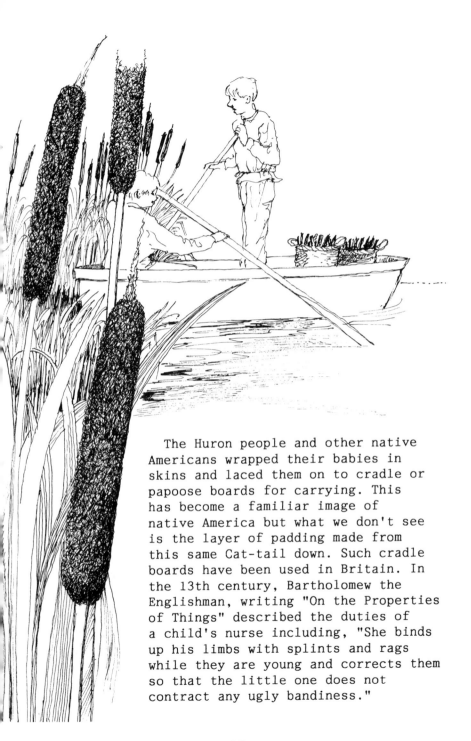

The Huron people and other native
Americans wrapped their babies in
skins and laced them on to cradle or
papoose boards for carrying. This
has become a familiar image of
native America but what we don't see
is the layer of padding made from
this same Cat-tail down. Such cradle
boards have been used in Britain. In
the 13th century, Bartholomew the
Englishman, writing "On the Properties
of Things" described the duties of
a child's nurse including, "She binds
up his limbs with splints and rags
while they are young and corrects them
so that the little one does not
contract any ugly bandiness."

MOSSES AND NAPPIES

The wren is said to have taken moss and feathers to line the manger at the Nativity, thereby receiving God's blessing and making it unlucky to kill one. In the 1960s in Surrey children, stalking the hedgerows with catapults, were warned that they would be cursed by God if they killed a wren. Formerly, it was right to kill a wren on Saint Stephen's Day (December 26th), for 'Hunting the Wren' practices, which involved Furze (Ulex europaeus) or Holly rather than moss. These ceremonies persisted longer in Ireland than the rest of the British Isles and appear to have had sacred origins, judging from the way the Church was still taking part in France in the early 19th century. The wren has more folk belief and traditional ritual attached to it than any other British bird.

It is not surprising that the wren was believed to have taken moss to the Nativity when its own nest is so beautifully constructed from the material. There are some 150 common mosses in Britain to choose from but very few have been found serviceable for household uses. Of those that have, the most important of these are the Bog Mosses of the genus Sphagnum, familiar to many readers as the filling for wreaths and the lining for hanging baskets. Such uses have brought the moss into serious decline and alternative materials should now be used.

The Sphagnums are among the largest of the mosses and grow in great spongy clumps on the wet heathlands and in bogs; so much so, that in some counties a boggy area is known as a 'moss'. As a raw material they are not only valuable for being available in bulk and for being so soft but because they are so water absorbent: after drying they will absorb up to sixteen times their own weight of water which is twice as much as does cotton. Nothing was better for lining a nappy. They were fairly safe too, being practically sterile from having grown in acid conditions.

Thus in 1995 came this letter from Lucy Baker, relating to Surrey:-

"I spoke to my mother about the use of Sphagnum moss in the nappies. My father was trained as a doctor at Guys Hospital just before the war. My mother was a nurse and health visitor in the early 1940s at Bletchingly near Godstone but I do not know if that was where she got the idea. As she said, "It's a long time ago now."

What she told me was that she collected the moss from around the lake in the Royal Military Academy grounds at Camberley (until the early 1970s there was free public access there). The moss was dried in the bottom oven of the Aga and then used. As far as my mother can remember she made a sort of nappy out of cloth with a pocket between the legs. The pocket was stuffed with the moss and the nappy pinned on. This was used when the baby was being potty trained and was a lot less bulky than a terry nappy. I think later on there were pants with a pocket in as well. The moss was incredibly absorbent stuff and soaked up the wee. When wet it was taken out and put on the compost heap. I can't say I remember this as I was the baby - this would have been in 1953/4."

The sterile nature and absorptive qualities of the Sphagnum mosses made them an excellent wound dressing for all ages. Further-more they have an antibiotic content and assist wound healing by way of the micro-organisms associated with them, including penicillium. Thus Bog Moss has been used by man since at least the Bronze Age right up to treating the casualties from the First World War. Now factory-made dressings are used and drugs administered to compensate for the loss of the healing properties.

The nappies themselves have traditionally been woven from linen, produced from the fibres of the flax plant since prehistoric times. For nappies it was an obvious choice when everyday cloth was either woollen or linen. The origins of the word 'nappy' go back through the French to the Latin. It had come into English by the early 15th century (earliest record 1420) but as linen table 'napkins'. It wasn't until 1845 that a napkin for babies got recorded (by the novelist Mrs Gaskell). When this became our familiar 'nappy' isn't known but the earliest use of it in print traced so far by the Oxford English Dictionary is only from 1927.

The alternative name was diaper, as used in the American language and which sounds oddly foreign to the English. However, it was once an English word, used for example by Shakespeare in 1596 in 'The Taming of the Shrew'. Originally that was not the name of the product but of a particular way of weaving. It produced a diamond pattern.

Diaper too comes from the French and ultimately from the Greek 'diaspros' meaning shining through white (aspros - white). As a weave, it was used for silk before linen so it really has come down the social scale!

Flax

GRIPE WATER

Now for three herbs that have a soothing effect on the digestive system and have been used for hundreds of years in 'gripe water' for easing wind out of babies.

Dill (Anethum graveolens) is a dainty annual with very finely cut ferny leaves and flat umbels of yellow flowers, which will grace any garden. Sadly it is now rarely grown but the seeds can be bought as a culinary herb. From it was made an infusion as 'dill water' for children's indigestion and flatulence. Of particular merit is the way it retains its valuable compounds after drying and in its seeds, making it available even when the fresh herb is out of season. The action of the 'oil of dill' comes from the carvone content (43-63%).

A very close relative is Fennel (Foeniculum vulgare), which looks the same but is far larger and is perennial. It "expels wind" observed John Evelyn in his salad book, "Acetaria: A Discourse of Sallets" of 1699, but it had already been used as a digestive aid in Britain since the Middle Ages. It had been popular as a cheap home-grown substitute for anise; they both contain the valuable compound, fenchone. True anise (Pimpinella anisum) prefers warmer summers than those of Britain and therefore supplies had to be imported, making them expensive, especially when subject to special taxation. For example, Edward I in 1305 taxed all such herbs and spices crossing London Bridge.

Like Dill the seeds yield a volatile oil but only 4% to 5%. in even the best strains. Thus it takes about 500kg of seeds to get 1kg of oil and that is mainly anethole, 50%-60%, while the much more desirable fenchone is only 18%-22%. Proportions vary according to the strain grown. Apparently the French have Fennel growing wild that contains only small amounts of the anethole, making them very bitter, and used in their 'Essence de Fenouil amer'.

British gripe water became a mixture of Fennel Oil
and sodium bicarbonate, sweetened with syrup, while
Fennel compounds were used for the 'Liquorice Powder'
so much used for griping earlier this century.

Both Dill and Fennel are 'warming' herbs and very
valuable when that is the desired effect. To cool the
baby down, reduce agitation etc. change to Peppermint.
Used since at least the 13th century, it was given
official recognition in the London Pharmacopoeia in the
first half of the 18th century. It is still retained in
many of the national pharmacopoeias today, being a very
valuable herb. The cooling compound is menthol, which
makes up some 50% of the volatile oil in the plant.

This cooling quality is very
soothing when applied as a
wound herb to children's
grazes etc. for which
the menthol provides
a disinfectant action.
No wonder it's used so
much in toothpaste.
When it comes to gripe
water, this mint version
is particularly good
to the lower bowel.

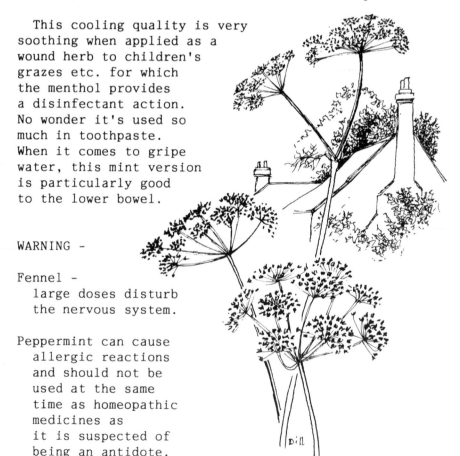

WARNING -

Fennel -
    large doses disturb
    the nervous system.

Peppermint can cause
    allergic reactions
    and should not be
    used at the same
    time as homeopathic
    medicines as
    it is suspected of
    being an antidote.

PAEONIES AND TEETHING

Come May time and the short stemmed old fashioned Paeonies with heavy globular crimson heads bow under the weight of sudden showers and bleed their petals over the edge of the grass. Although not native, these grand plants, introduced from the Continent, have been here for many centuries. Originally, with single rather than double blooms it was one of the grandest flowers of the medicinal herb garden, sought by rich and poor alike:- in 1275 the king's agent was buying roots at two shillings while in the next century the 'Piers Plowman' poem includes the lines:

"Hast thou, quoth he, any hot spices?
         I have pepper and paeony seeds and
                  a pound of garlick
          and a farthingworth of fennel-seed,
                  for fasting days."

The seeds were a valued spice and remained so until the 18th century; as late as 1796 Mrs Glasse's Cookery directed "Stick the cream with Paeony kernels". By this time its prime use as a medicinal plant was also in decline especially as suspicions were growing that it might be toxic. Authorities are still not agreed upon this. It certainly contains powerful irritants so that a child eating only three or four petals is liable to vomit, so it is usually classified as poisonous and should be respected as such.

In the past, however, it has played important roles in rearing children. At teething time sections of root were threaded onto a string and worn as a necklace so that baby could bite on it. The roots are the most powerful part of the plant and have in them a compound that helps to stop bleeding. However, THIS SHOULD NOT BE TRIED TODAY. The same facility may well have been exploited by the mother at the time of the birth of the baby, for Paeonia preparations were used "for women who are not sufficiently cleansed after childbirth," (Culpeper). Today the herb has declined

29

to just seven preparations in the British Pharmacopoeia (1993) two of which are still for the vascular system. Another reason to hang the roots of a Paeony round the neck of a child was to cure it of the 'falling sickness'. Adults needed to drink down a preparation in wine and even then it was only considered effective if taken at the onset of the trouble. An alternative remedy for the 'falling sickness' was from the Corn Poppies (Papaver rhoeas); so said Matthiolus and duly confirmed by Culpeper.

Anyone digging up a Paeony by daylight will have their eyes pecked out by a woodpecker. That may sound just a little unbelievable but by training young herbalists to gather it at night the profession kept the identity of this very valuable medicine a secret, and, should it become known, then there was a built in deterrent to anyone intent on getting their own for free. These considerations were all important when we remember that Paeonies are not easy to crop as they are slow to get their roots established and yet it's the thick older roots that are the most desirable. Some were worn round children's necks as an amulet to protect against evil.

In the same way they were used to drive away the disturbing spirits that caused nightmares and bad dreams. Persistent dreams were treated with a medicine made from the seeds which are so shiny they were said to glow in the dark, giving rise to the belief that the plant was specially created by the gods. Thus shepherds adopted it to protect themselves and their flocks from the predators of the night and it was even tried for protecting the harvest from storms.

More scientific, to our way of thinking, was its use against childhood convulsions, which was valid. The plant contains compounds that soothe spasms - if used correctly and one of the seven preparations in the British Pharmacopoeia is for just this purpose. Old notions of laying the freshly dug roots on the soles of an epileptic child or upon the chest of a sleeping lunatic do not sound very convincing as cures.

Finally, for gardeners who wonder which species is being discussed - wonder on! The answer is far from clear but the earliest records (from late Saxon) refer probably to Paeonia mascula (the male paeony of Gerard) and become superseded (mid 16thC?) by P. officinalis (the female). The double form is P.o.'rubra plena'. The popular garden hybrids are derived from P.lactiflora.

Paeonia officinalis
'rubra plena'

Paeonia mascula
Dig one up and a woodpecker will fly down and peck out your eyes.

SWEETS AND CABBAGES

Sweeties for the children, for good or bad, have been very much part of the post-war affluence. Sugar is by no means new and has an interesting story, that weaves through wars and religions and slavery. It commences some 5,000 years ago when Sugar Cane was being harvested in its tropical homelands, while in the cold north honey was the main sweetener. By the 12th century imports of Arabic sugar from Sugar Cane were already in demand as an expensive luxury. Once the plant had been taken to the New World and cropping established in Brazil and the West Indies supplies increased. That was in the early 16th century. In 1545, Robert Reneger, a Southampton merchant and shipowner, became the first Englishman to capture a Spanish treasure ship, the San Salvador, as she returned from the West Indies. Apart from the gold and silver and pearls, the booty also included 124 chests of sugar. No doubt that was very profitable as it coincided with a period of high inflation and sugar was one of the hard hit luxuries. From Henry VIII's proclamation of 1544 we learn that the price of sugar had risen sharply from 3d or 4d per pound to 9d and 10d; he set the price for even the best sugar at 7d. By the end of the century ports like Norwich had a booming trade in such luxury goods, so that the number of grocers trading in the city had doubled since the mid 1520s. English trade had changed greatly since the beginning of the century when wool merchants attending the great continental fairs spent part of their profits abroad, on luxuries to trade back home. Thus William Mucklow of Worcester in 1511 bought two tons of sugar on such an expedition to Holland. (See Youings and Lewington)

A glance into Georgian recipe books reveals pounds and pounds of the stuff being poured into cream desserts in a way that would horrify any dietitian today! As long ago as 2,800 BC Sugar Cane was being grown as a staple in India and lumps of processed sugar being eaten as 'Khanda' from which the American 'candy' derives.

Norfolk Sugar Beet Field 1981

First successful British
Sugar Beet factory built
at Cantley, Norfolk, 1912.

34

Meanwhile, a separate story was unfolding, namely the development of root crops. From the genus Beta came a range of 'beets' including a very sweet one which the Romans had started using as a vegetable. This became the Sugar Beet but getting worthwhile amounts out of the root was a different matter. The technical problem was solved in 1748 by the German scientist Andreas Marggraf and in 1799 the first factory was built at Breslau.

The next great stimulus to development came with the Napoleonic Wars. Britain interrupted France's imports of cane sugar and so Napoleon turned attention to the possibility of becoming self-sufficient with beet sugar. Benjamin Delessoret of the French Academy of Science tackled the task and was hailed as the first to refine Sugar Beet commercially, for which he was decorated by Napoleon with the Legion of Honour in 1812. It was then decreed that French farmers should grow Sugar Beet, for which Napoleon provided State assistance. He also banned imports of cane sugar which not only helped home production but hit Britain's financial interests in the trade of the West Indies.

The New World sugar plantations were of course worked by slaves and so the Quakers now enter the story. They were among the first to oppose slavery and so to undermine the system they started Britain's first Sugar Beet factory in 1832. At the same time beet growing was expanding in Central and Eastern Europe, reducing demand for cane sugar, and with the eventual abolition of slavery throughout the British Empire in 1833, prices rose sharply. British trade suffered and so in 1874 Gladstone was forced to lift taxation on sugar. This made sugar affordable to the lower income groups and with that came the development of commercially produced confectionery.

(prime sources British Sugar plc; Food From Britain)

Some other plants taste sweeter than sugar. One in particular tastes many times so, due its high content of glycyrrhizin (calcium and potassium salts of glycyrrhinic acid) and therefore of importance to diabetics. This wonder plant is Liquorice. There are about fourteen members of the genus but only a few have the sweet roots of value to commerce. In Western Europe a Middle Eastern species is used, Glycyrrhiza glabra, which has been used for medicines and confectionary for thousands of years. The Scythians are thought to have used it first and given the knowledge to the Greeks who called it Scythian Root. It is referred to by Theophrastus in the 3rd century BC and was known to Dioscorides who coined the name of the genus from the Greek words for 'sweet' and 'root'.

For some peculiar reason liquorice has never been very popular in England. It was known widely in 11th century Germany (as a medicine) and yet it is not until 1264 that we find an English record - an entry in the Wardrobe Accounts of Henry IV. That would have been for imported material. It took us a long time to get round to growing it ourselves. Italy was growing it by the 13th century and John Harvey in his 'Medieval Gardens' thinks it probably reached here in the 14th century but the date most often given is 1562. That's when Turner published his herbal and recorded home cultivation but Stow reported "the planting and growing of licorish began about the first year of Queen Elizabeth" and that was 1558. From field name evidence John Field believes it was here by late medieval times, with which the Royal Horticultural Society concurs. Perhaps it was a rarity given a boost by foreign Huguenot immigrants.

Interestingly it is not mentioned by Walter Blyth in "The English Improver" of 1649 but was included three years later when he published "The English Improver Improved".

By the 17th century is was grown widely, from Dorset up to Shropshire, Cheshire and so to Yorkshire where it became famous around Pontefract, where they still make the confectionary today (from imported liquorice). Tradition around Pontefract (alias Pomfrey of Pomfrey Cakes fame) has the business beginning in Elizabethan times but John Harvey (see Early Nurserymen) cannot locate evidence older than the early 1700s. The 1735 Irish herbal of John K'Eogh made its status plain:

"It is planted by us in gardens, and is brought to great perfection in my Lord Kingstons Gardens at Mitchelstown, where the root may be seen as thick as a man's finger. It is extraordinary pleasant to the taste, far exceeding what is commonly brought to us from foreign countries, so you see, how by a little industry, the most exotic plants may be brought to perfection in this country, which demonstrates what a fertile, prolific land we live in.
The virtues of this plant are so well known, almost to everyone that I need not enlarge much upon it. The roots are beneficial for coughs and obstructions of the lungs; they also provoke urine, break up stone and are good for the liver and disorders of the mouth."

Judging from the other evidence he was about right (although unaware of the side-effects of over indulgence as a medicine - see Mills and Martindale) and our liquorice was indeed said to have the best flavour of all. The product is made from the roots which are quite massive for a herbaceous plant - but what a plant! From the root cuttings that were first planted it grew bigger each year - one foot, two foot, until in fourth year it could reach five feet high. Then it was harvested so that the roots could be boiled to extract and refine the compounds that make commercial liquorice. Four years is a long wait for a return but each acre yielded 4-5 tons and prices were so good it was worth it. As the rows had to be spaced 3-4 feet apart there was room for a cash crop to be grown between; potatoes and cabbages were popular as they liked the heavy manuring necessary for the liquorice. For this reason it was usually grown near towns, where the horses provided plenty of dung. Now we no longer grow it.

A herb that is still popular, and which contains the same glycyrrhizin is Sweet Cicely. It is especially effective for removing the tartness of desserts such as rhubarb, whether by adding roots or stems and for this reason is valuable today for diabetics. It is very easy to grow, quickly producing large fanged roots and sweet ferny leaves which appear early in the spring. They tend to yellow off by midsummer but if the plant is cut down and kept watered a fresh crop appears and lasts into the frosts. It now grows wild from Britain across to the Caucasus, but it is not known whether it is truly native to Britain. Authorities have their doubts and it is not recorded by Godwin from pre-historic records. Native or not it is a very attractive multi-purpose plant for any garden whether or not you concur with the old belief that feeding the boiled roots to children will promote their strength and courage!

Before cheap sweets other plants were offered to children between meals, including cabbage stalks. Now if there's one thing that children are, traditionally, not supposed to relish is cabbage. Boiled school greens have seen to that! Even before the invention of school dinners children in the workhouses learned to loath cabbage as it could be adulterated with Burdock leaves. These are mucilaginous and difficult to swallow and quite disgusting! Fresh raw cabbage on the other hand is a different matter and the stalks were the 'sweets' of George Sturt in the 1860s:-

> "But I did often enjoy cabbage-stumps, which my
> mother cut from the cabbages she was preparing
> for dinner, and put (for me) in a glass of water
> on the window-sill of the wash-house..."

Another sweet, marshmallow, has much in common with liquorice, in the sense that they both come from plants that were brought into use for their medicinal value. The true Marshmallow plant is Althaea officinalis. The generic name Althaea comes from the Greek 'altho' meaning to cure and the specific name, officinalis, means it was recognised officially as a medicine. It is the best in a very large family of healing plants. In some instances, however, people and books refer to Marshmallow when Common Mallow is meant; that's a close relative Malva sylvestris, having bright pinkish purple flowers with darker stripes rather than the beautiful white blooms of the Althaea, to be found by the sea.

There's more confusion over its origins: whether it is native or comes from China. If it was introduced then it was long ago; it occurs several times in the early archaeological record (see Godwin), it was one of the herbs used by the Welsh physicians of Myddfai in the 13th century and is thought to be one of the plants carved on the misericords of Wells Cathedral in the 14th century - long before other mallows from China were introduced.

To make the original marshmallow confection take the roots that are over two years old, dry them, powder them, soak in water for eight hours. It turns into mucilage which is then heated with sugar. Originally lumps were used as 'throat sweets' for respiratory problems and it does the whole digestive system good too. The pleasantness of this and liquorice when most other medicines tasted dreadful explains their wide popularity. It also made them acceptable to children, especially as its action is so gentle and soothing. The Persians are thought to have been the first to use it to reduce inflammation when babies were teething. They also said it encouraged late-developing teeth. In Britain the roots were used as teething rings - much tastier and safer than the old toxic Paeony roots.

Today's confection, sold as marshmallow has never been near a root! It is basically starch and gum and sweetener.

Marsh Mallows 1981

Something else that has changed from its natural
origins is the Easter Egg. Originally real eggs were
used, as part of the pagan fertility rites for the
veneration of Oestre who was held responsible for the
regeneration of spring life. This was too important to
be overthrown by the early missionaries and so it was
Christianised as Easter but many of the old practices
persisted. Among these was the use of Easter Eggs which
were not then child-orientated. For example, King Edward
I (r.1272-1307) on one occasion needed 400 eggs for
his Easter celebrations at Court.

These were all dyed and needed to be the traditional
colour for fertility which was green. To this end all
the eggs would have been rubbed with the petals of the
beautiful Pasque Flower (Anemone pulsatilla now
Pulsatilla vulgaris). Although such dyeing was pagan in
origin the flower had been Christianised with the
belief that it hangs its flowers in remembrance of
having been growing on Calvary at the time of the
Crucifixion and that it now raises its head on Easter
Day to show off its grand corona of golden stamens
that symbolise the glorious Resurrection.

This wild flower is now scarce having been collected
as cut flowers, grubbed up for garden use, gathered
for herbal medicine and stripped of its petals for
dyeing. At least the development of synthetic dyes last
century began to take some of the pressure off. At the
same time real eggs changed to chocolate eggs through
the changes in the sugar industry. In particular the
Quaker connection led to the Cadbury brothers founding
the chocolate production for which the name is still
famous today. Many a reader must remember the hope of
getting a Cadbury's chocolate egg for Easter, wrapped
smartly in its coloured foil. For this the base colour
was green again as the tradition of green Easter eggs
persisted into modern industrial production. There was
still a nostalgic delight in real eggs though and that
persisted well into this century, when for example, the
Model Dairy at Caterham in Surrey was still delivering
chicken eggs dyed green in 1935.

Pasque Flower
(Pulsatilla vulgaris)
For dyeing Easter Eggs

GOOD BEHAVIOUR

You can tell some children not to do something until you are blue in the face. Then, as soon as your back is turned they go and do it again. One way of extending your control is to frighten them from continuing with the activity or to frighten them away from the place. It makes good sense. A flooded clay pit or a river bank can be a deep and dangerous place to play around, but, if children are assured that the site is inhabited by an evil being, such as Yorkshire's 'Jenny Greenteeth', who will grab children off the bank and drag them down underwater to drown, then maybe the children will keep away. There were countless local 'bogies' around the country who deterred children from dangerous places.

The same idea could be used for crop protection. Ripe fruit has always been a favourite and children still 'scrump' apples. This verb is not derived from the 'scrump' or little shrivelled apples used for scrumpy cider but from another dialect word from which we get the Standard English word 'scrimp'.

44

A contributor remembered that in the late 1950s at the fruit farm at Bramley in Surrey the children were warned that if they came for fruit on a Sunday then a big brown hairy hand would come out of the branches and throttle them. This sounds very much like a deterrent from stealing the fruit on a Sunday when there were no staff around. I am told that the notion of the big brown hairy hand is ancient and that one of its strongholds has been North Wales. Interestingly, Lloyd George, who had a house at Churt in Surrey, brought Welsh workers to the village to start the fruit farms there. It's only a few miles from Churt to Bramley.

It's not a great step from these notions to those that say the plant itself will do harm; not plants like Stinging Nettles and Brambles, but plants that would otherwise be thought perfectly harmless.

The most interesting of these is the Corn Poppy (Papaver rhoeas). It has not always been regarded as fearsome. To the ancient cultures - Assyrian, Egyptian, Greek and Roman - it was held in high esteem or even considered sacred while here the Romano-British must have had similar beliefs as we know it was used at funerals. In terms of its veneration it has been one of the prime symbols of fertility and of an after-life. By the 1980s when a reduction in the use of herbicides brought swathes of poppies back to the countryside numerous people remembered that they were 'necessary' for the "good health of the land" or for the "good health of the crops". So why do we find that in some regions children were warned to fear them and not to pick them? If you pick poppies you will be struck by lightning or by

a thunder bolt; picking poppies will make you go
blind; pick poppies and you'll get pains in the head.
These were such frequent warnings that the very poppy
itself became known by such local names as Lightnings,
Thunderballs, Thunderbolts, Thunderclaps and Thunder-
flower; Blind Eyes, Blindman and Blindybuffs; also
Headache. It has been suggested that the last came
from using the narcotic poppy as an analgesic but
that in turn has been countered by statements that
the drug content in British poppies is too slight to
be effective. Apparently staring at the vibrant red
does upset the visual senses in some people.

Such dire warnings
seem to be aimed at
stopping the children
from trampling down
the corn prior to
harvesting as they
push through to reach
the pretty flowers.
Although there were
other tempting flowers
such as the Cornflower,
Corn Cockle and Corn
Marigold it is the
poppy that is liable
to drop its petals when
picked and thereby
encourage the children
deeper into the corn in
search of more resilient
blooms.

One reason for wanting the
blooms was for the making of
little lady dolls in scarlet
dresses. Pick a poppy with
enough stem to become a leg.
Turn the petals down to make
a dress and tie a waist into
the top third with a piece of
grass and to secure a second
leg from another length of
poppy stem. Push another piece
of stem between the petals to
make a pair of arms and finally
remove a section of stamens as
a haircut to suggest her face.

Poppy petals were used as a truth flower by young
lovers. A fallen petal was placed over the chink left
when the index finger is curled inside the thumb in a
loosely clenched hand. Then the petal is smacked smartly
by bringing down the free hand upon it. The two lovers
must do this simultaneously. If both petals pop then
their love is true. If only one child's petal pops then
the other child has awkward questions to answer. If
neither petal pops then obviously "it's no good" and a
second pair are gathered; true love doesn't die that
easily!

An alternative truth flower was any of the yellow
buttercups. It is well known that a bloom held under a
child's chin will reflect gold on the skin. This was
used widely to indicate whether the child liked butter
or not but the practice was also used to test whether
the child was telling the truth or not. Dirty skin does
not reflect the gold of course, so, was this the origin
of the expression "dirty liar"? The Oxford English
Dictionary has no recorded origin for this expression,
believing 'dirty' was used simply for emphasis.

47

SPARE THE ROD

"That in the year 1869, there should be living in England and in London, a considerable number of women, many apparently in good society, and some of them titled, who are in the regular habit of stripping and flogging with birches, apple-twigs, or leather straps, their daughters of thirteen years old and upward, must appear to foreigners incredible, and to most Englishmen very queer...They seem to glory in the privilege of thrashing their girls ."

From The Saturday Review; 1869

There had been months of correspondence leading up to the above observation so the periodical knew the state of affairs well. Although many agreed with this dissenting voice things were very slow to change. In 1900 more than 30,000 children younger than sixteen were birched. In 1915 a boy of eight was given six strokes of the birch for setting fire to a tree in the park. This was despite the 1908 'Childrens' Charter' having made young children less responsible for their criminal behaviour. No longer were they to be sent to adult prisons but to special insitutions of their own, such as reformatories and industrial schools. This put a stigma on all institutions set up to help the needy, even those, of course, that would only consider taking those who had no criminal record.

Birch catkins enlarged.

Things still have not changed very much and foreigners still "find it incredible" that we should feel the need for corporal punishment in schools, that mothers should thrash their children and that we could have a great debate in the mid 1990s as to whether child-minders should have the right to strike the children in their care. The Isle of Man is the last place in the British Isles to keep birching as an official legal punishment although it hasn't been used for some years now. There is the fear that to do so would bring a hearing in the European Court of Human Rights and that they would lose. Nevertheless the Birch rods are renewed each year as per time immemorial.

Birching is so old it is prehistoric. By Roman times officials called lictors preceded the consul (high magistrate) into court, bearing their insignia of office - their 'fasces', meaning bundles. These were axes bound round with Birch stems so as not to obscure the blade, suggesting that these signified the two options, either capital or corporal punishment. Apparently archaeologists have unearthed similar things from mesolithic times. Certainly by Celtic times the Birch was well established as a tree of great symbolic use. It beat out evil and beat in goodness, or, in the case of birch brooms, swept them in and out. Thus at the end of the Celtic year there was a ceremonial sweeping out of the old year, leaving a clean welcome for the new. That time is known today as Hallowe'en and children in infant schools still make silhouettes of the old year's evil as 'witches' flying off on the birch broomsticks.

Another ancient practice was teaching children the boundary of their territory which has come down to us as 'beating the bounds'. They were taken around the lands by their elders and at the boundary markers they were beaten so that they would not forget the spot. That became Christianised to mark out the parish boundaries but in due course the ritual birching was dropped. Some parishes have revived the occasion but not the beating of course!

COUNTING OUT

"He loves me. He loves me not. He loves me....." and another petal is plucked from the Daisy flower. There are numerous ways children measure their counting and in view of ancient religious significance given to the Daisy as a protector of children, this particular way could be very old. It is just one of many ways of 'counting out' to try to foretell the future in love and marriage and there's enough of those to fill a book. Another version, known widely, predicts the way the girl will be transported at the church for her wedding, ranging from a carriage to a dung cart.

After flower petals, the most popular counters were fruit stones. Again these were used by girls to predict their futures husband: tinker, tailor, soldier, sailor, rich man, poor man, beggar man, thief. This game was not scorned so loudly by the boys as they used versions of it to predict their occupation. This was popular after the Second World War when school dinners offered a weekly dish of prunes that was soon encircled with stones perched on the broad rims of the plates. It's all harmless fun, although at times it can test the sense of humour! There is a serious side in that some were designed to teach young children to count in numbers, while others were occupational rhymes such as those employed by the lace-makers to ensure youngsters workers didn't get lost in the complicated sequences.

The rhymes get updated with the changing times and therefore could be very ancient in their origins. Counting in 'five bar gates', that is, with four vertical marks crossed through diagonally with the fifth marker, has been found on a French cave wall from the end of the last Ice Age. On the other hand, telling the time with a Dandelion 'clock' must be as recent as when clocks became common and the day began to be finely divided into hourly intervals. For any- not initiated into this timepiece, the number of puffs it takes to blow all the seeds off the stalk equals the number of hours passed on the clock.

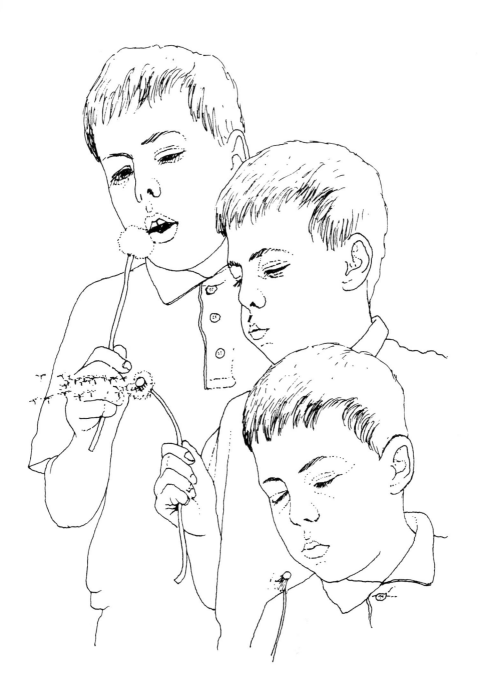

Tom Bourne
Courtesy Worplesdon County Primary School, Surrey.

51

PLANTAIN SOLDIERS

The common weed of roadsides and coarse grassy areas known as Ribwort Plantain (Plantago lanceolata) was once an important plant in medieval horticulture, where it was grown for use in herbal medicines and today is still listed in eleven preparations in the British Pharmacopoeia. These are all for respiratory disorders as has always been its main use.

It also provides the material for an ancient game. Children taking the black flower heads for the playing of 'soldiers'. That's as widespread as is the plant - right across Europe into Central and Northern Asia. Where the plant has been taken to other temperate areas so the game has gone with it to most of them.

For those not initiated into this game, each of two combatants takes turns to hold out a flowering stalk while the other attempts to strike off its head with that of his own stalk. When a combatant loses his head and then he is obviously the loser but to prolong the game, armed forces of plantain heads are gathered and annihilated one by one until the best team wins. It's easiest if combatants strike at right angles to each other but to show off greater eye-hand co-ordination, combatants should face each other.

This Plantain has over five dozen English names, among which is Kemps or Kempers, derived probably from the Saxon word 'cempa' for a fighting man and thereby giving some idea of the antiquity of the game. In some northern dialects there is still the verb 'to kemp', meaning to fight, and there are parallels in other N.W. European languages. An early reference to the game relates to 1152, although it wasn't written down until later, in a verse biography not completed until 1226. It's the life of William the Marshall, written in French by John D'Erley at the instigation of William's eldest son. It has survived because William rose through the ranks to become King's regent and the epitome of early medieval chivalry.

52

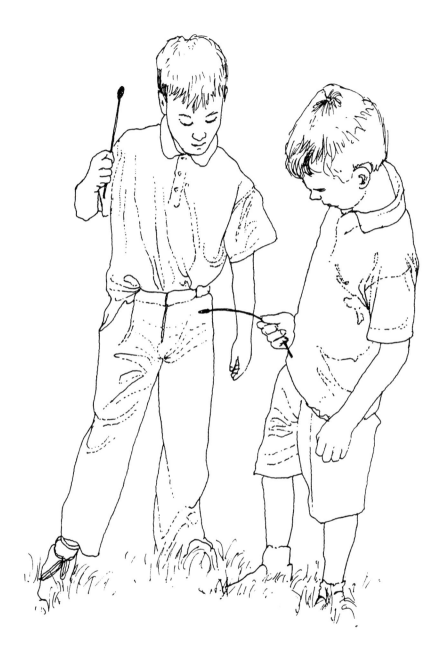

Tom Bourne and Daniel Maddison
Courtesy Worplesdon County Primary School, Surrey.

We read in this, "L'Histoire de Guillaume Merachel"
that William's father, John, served King Stephen in
the wars against Matilda but changed sides when she
started to win. He was trapped in Newbury Castle in
1152 while defending it against the beseiging forces
of King Stephen. He was, however, granted safe passage
to go and confer with Matilda - but on condition that
he gave up one of his sons as a hostage to ensure his
safe return. William, the youngest, aged between six
and nine, was chosen and handed over. John returned in
defiant mood and continued resisting King Stephen's
forces who then threatened the life of his son. John
retorted that he "had the anvils and hammers with
which to forge finer sons."

William was taken out to be hanged but was reprieved
by the king. The seige persisted. Then it was proposed
to catapult the boy over the castle wall but the King
once more reprieved him and guaranteed his safety. For
two months William remained King Stephen's prisoner
and one day we read that William challenged the King
to a game of "chevaliers" with the Plantains among the
hay used for strewing in the tent. Stephen held out
his 'knight' and the boy promptly struck off its head,
so Stephen had to offer up another, as per the rules
of the game...but then the discovery of a spy in the
camp interrupted the contest. Stephen was censured for
allowing one of his enemies to taste sweet victory
over him! The boy was eventually returned safely to
his parents.   [see Frances Gies, pp.99-101]

There is a whole range of English country
names of a martial nature for the Ribwort
Plantain. These include Black Jacks, Cocks
and Hens and other cock variants, Fetchers
or Fighters, Fighting Cocks, Headman, Men
of War, Swords and Spears. The name Lances
sounds martial but is a catch, referring to
the shape of the leaves, which were used
for human food, animal fodder and medicine.
The names Conker or Conqueror are better
known in connection with Horse
Chestnuts described next.

Ribwort Plantains with the present Manor house at Stoke D'Abernon, Surrey, where, in an earlier house, William the Marshall spent his honeymoon - the earliest record of a honeymoon.

PLAYING CONKERS

The game of 'soldiers' will remind many readers of playing 'conkers' or 'conquerors' with the fruits, known as conkers, of the Horse Chestnut (Aesculus hippocastanum) or Conker Tree. It's very simple. The large nuts are threaded onto a string (or a willow twig in earlier times), and then two combatants strike one upon the other in turn until one breaks, leaving the other the 'conqueror'. There are standardised ways in which each player holds his string and in some regions there are rhymes with which to initiate the contest or to choose who strikes first. A new rule has been enforced by some schools, concerned about the mess of the broken conkers all over the playground, namely that the loser has the job of picking up the pieces and putting them in the waste bin.

This, however, isn't a particularly old game, unless it's true that it was played earlier with snail shells and that the name therefore comes from 'conch'. The tree itself has only been in the country 400 years. It is a native of Albania and Greece but its date of introduction is not known for certain; the dates 1577, 1600 and 1616 occur in the debates. The most popular story has the great botanist Clusius receiving seeds from his friend the Austrian Ambassador to the Sultan of Turkey in Constantinople. Clusius was in Vienna at the time and, as with other plants new to the west, he distributed these seeds to various European contacts. John Evelyn, on the other hand, acknowledged the above route, adds that to England it came direct from the Levant, but gives no date, (Silva, Book I, Ch.VIII).

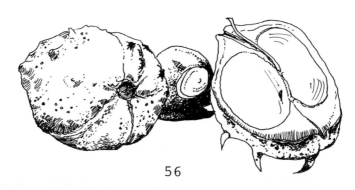

Horse Chestnut

It arrived as a source of important horse medicine, hence its name, but was soon appreciated as one of the grandest of ornamental trees. Through all seasons it provides beauty and interest but in May it bears great panicles, up to 30cm high, of white blooms with a yellow eye that turns pink, each being some 2cm across and therefore very showy. A lot of these are male blooms and the rest are hermaphrodite so only a few are fertilized and start growing into little spiny fruits. Of these perhaps only two or three will mature into the great green fruits, to come crashing down and split open into pure white cases for the polished mahogany seeds that are the 'conkers'.

As for the childhood game, that is recorded from only scattered localities even in the second half of the 19th century. The Oxford English Dictionary gives 1877 as the earliest written record. George Sturt wrote of playing it in the 1860s (Small Boy in the Sixties, p.159) but that wasn't published until 1927. However, once invented it seems to have spread rapidly, and not just in the countryside, since the tree was popular for planting in streets and city parks. It did not prove very suitable for streets since, in due course, boughs had to be lopped and many started to rot back from the wounds, creating a fresh hazard.

Collecting the fruit presents its own hazards to people and vehicles in the vicinity of the trees. The harvesters hurl missiles into the branches. These are to bring down the unripe fruits and all attention is upon these rather than passing traffic since they must be caught before they hit the ground. Caught conkers are more highly prized, and rightly so, since hitting the ground can weaken the nut. There's a lot of esteem involved in having a champion conker. Each takes its name from the number of opponents it has smashed - a sixer is not unusual but a tenner is getting top of the range and raises suspicions. It is most likely to be sniffed vigorously for any whiff of vinegar since it is strictly against the rules to harden them over-night by pickling. Similarly they mustn't be baked. That shows up by the conkers losing their shine.

Childhood games ran in seasonal cycles and playing conkers has for several generations been the game that opened the autumn term at school. Increasingly they're being left to strew the autumn paths, apparently of unknown worth. Children no longer know the distinctive raw smell of the borings as the meat skewer drills the string-hole (but then what are meat skewers?!). It has become the adults who are keeping the game alive by organising championships to raise money for charity.

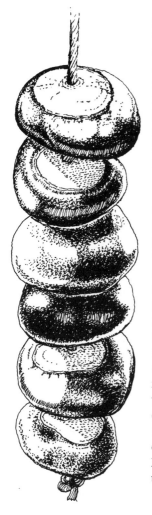

It is perhaps worth adding that the game remains very British and is unknown in many of the countries where the tree has been introduced, although it is played in its native regions. The game is barely known in the United States and yet they have their own red-flowered species, called Buckeyes. Admittedly these have softer, smaller nuts that are less suitable for the game.

Sturt went on to describe another conker activity, known in his S.W. Surrey as 'mounters' as it still was a century later. He explained, "A 'mounter' was only a conqueror whirled round and round and at last sent mounting up into the sky. I don't know that there was anything in this game except the pleasure of seeing the thing go up, with its trailing string; yet the horse-chestnut tree often went by the name "mounter" tree, at the season when one was raking with one's feet over all the white and green debris to find, if possible, one more chestnut for one's long string at home. Chestnuts were so beautiful, until the gloss went off."

Strung for carrying

TAKING UP ARMS

"Gas him! Gas him!" came the call of our commander as we crouched out of sight, blow-pipes to our lips, mouths full of agasses. Another innocent victim came under attack. By the 1950s and 60s households no longer had sacks of dried peas to arm pea-shooters but the countryside provided its own armaments.

Agasses were the fruits of the Hawthorn and are now generally called 'haws' but back in the 1950s and 60s in S.W.Surrey we still used the derivative of the Saxon name 'haga'. With variations in spelling, it was the same all over the southern counties where the old Saxon kingdoms had been: agars in general for Surrey, Sussex and Hampshire, ag-garzes up in Buckinghamshire and agog in Berkshire, to aglet or eglet down in Devon and over the border into Celtic Cornwall with aglets, aglan and awglen. Many a district can provide its own peculiar variation. By 1954 at least one writer was declaring that the word was out of use. Not so. We gassed the milkman regularly. He would accelerate wonderfully - in our direction!

The blow-pipes were hand made of course. Sections of bamboo, cut between the nodes, were ideal as the length was just right for slipping into the back pocket. They had to be of a large species in order to get a bore wide enough to take the agass. Such stems were stolen quietly from old Victorian gardens. British substitutes are few. The only tree with hollow stems is the Elder but that tasted horrible and caused arguments as to whether it was unlucky to cut it.

There are not many herbaceous plants with rigid hollow stems. A few of the umbellifer family have been used, such as Cow Parsley. That has only a small bore so its fame far outweighs its true usage. Hemlock is well documented but again is unlikely to have been used much since country children were shown the purple spots "of death" on the stems and frightened off this lethal plant. The Greeks used it to kill Socrates in 399 BC.

The way the name Hemlock is used indiscriminately for other members of the same family adds further doubt to its use. Giant Hogweed, on the other hand, has received much press coverage in recent years since children have suffered terribly after using it for pea-shooters. The sap causes severe blistering and pain around the mouth, especially after the skin has been further exposed to sunlight. Teach children not to handle the plant at all. It is not a native but was introduced as a garden plant from the Caucasus in 1893. Having now escaped from the gardens it is increasing in the wild but under the Wildlife and Countryside Act 1981 it is illegal to plant it or cause it to grow in the countryside.

Being shot with agasses is not life-threatening but getting caught can be, and you do need to get rather close for real effectiveness with a pea-shooter. There were more subtle ways of using agasses. They made 'itching powder'. It was taken to school and dropped discreetly down the neck of the child sitting in front. Perhaps it would be unwise to describe precisely which part of the fruit was separated out for this quiet torment. Soon the delighted offender saw the victim's arm curl up the back to scratch between the shoulder blades or go into the arm over the shoulder contortion. A sharp, "Do sit still child," from the teacher was especially satisfying and signalled the need for the innocent look.

Audiences at presentations in Sussex have been putting forward the use of rose hips instead of agasses. Apparently they were more effective.

We children guarded our 'camps' with home-made bows and arrows in what seemed like timeless tradition that stretched back to Robin Hood at the very least. As it happened I was Davy Crockett the day I was challenged to show off my marksmanship; everyone was terribly impressed - not because I hit the target but that my father bled real blood. These certainly weren't toys and never had been. Bows and arrows and wooden swords have devolved from the days when fathers gave them to sons, and taught them to use them, as tangible signs of their increasing maturity - at an age when our present day children are more likely to be attending infant school.

The English and Welsh bowman of the Middle Ages were the most feared of fighting forces. They prowess was in part dependent upon the skill of the bowyers and fletchers. Their work had to be flawless - not just to ensure the release of an opponent's soul but for the conservation of the marksman's own. They are famed for working with Yew wood, taken from the trunks of the trees, not the branches. Trunk wood was expensive for the king, let alone children, and in our later days it was the Hazel tree that armed the feints of childhood battles. The suckers or 'wands' arising from a coppice stool were taken for both bows and for arrows and were the best available, providing straight, ready-made shafts, endowed with great tensile strenth that would persist as the wood dried out. Attempts to make 'real' bows out of Yew branches are doomed to failure as they are too flexible and lacking the necessary tensile power to spring back straight and propel arrows.

Hazels
Matherry 95

WOODEN TOYS

While boys of more wealthy households were being intiated into their martial responsibilities the girls were learning equestrian skills. The nursery rocking horse of Georgian and Victorian times had more serious beginnings than whiling away a wet afternoon. Similarly the roundabout horses at fairgrounds once galloped past poles bearing hoops that required their riders to lean out and snatch. That was a skill taken from medieval tournament fields but modern safety regulations have banished it to the history books.

The first rocking horses were in existence by the 1600s and are thought to have evolved out of rocking cradles as another way of soothing a fractious but older child. The earliest of these horses are thought to have been created out of oaken boards cut into silhouettes with rounded rocking base and a round log seat between them and a wooden head fixed in the gap.

Next came horses on curved bow rockers and these are truly three dimensional carved horses. The bodies were, ideally, of a light wood if possible, so that nanny could move it. The main starting point, however, was far away from an English nursery, up in the mountains of Switzerland, Austria, Italy, France and Germany. Here toy-making became a major activity as winter-work, for individual craftsmen during the long dark snow-bound days and nights. Trade fairs started of which Nuremburg became pre-eminent and has retained its leading place in the toy industry of today.

Materials were those at hand - the conifers of the mountains - until wooden horse production had expanded into new areas. Then the strength and lightness of the Beech was exploited for the legs, as in chairs. The bow rockers came to be made of Elm where its naturally twisted grain gave extra strength.

64

Designs followed fashions in real horsemanship and
so there was a ready demand for new models harnessed
with the latest tack or in imitation of the latest
breeds, champions, or royal purchase. To avoid losing
their market lead the German government organised their
trade at an early date, with agents, called Verlegers,
to mastermind it all. England, not to be beaten, turned
to the United States for help with production and so
many American rocking horses look English. The main
innovation was the change from rocking to swinging
horses on fixed bases and that was a safety measure,
since fingers and toes could be trapped under rockers.
They also damaged carpets and wooden floors, while the
the wall plaster got a hammering from any ill-placed
horse. The most successful of these new designs was
patented in January 1880 by P.J.Marqua of Cincinatti.
He called it a 'hobby horse' which was a name in use
by the 1750s for all wooden horses. Originally such
things were just heads on sticks, as theatrical props,
for Morris Dancers and Mummers, medieval miracle play
performers and all folk theatre round the world to
China.   (additional inf. see Stevenson & Marsden)

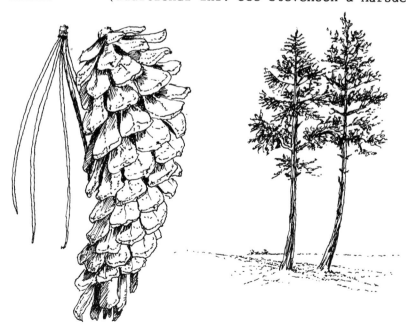

Pinus strobus.

65

The Rocking Horse Workshop at Wem, Shropshire, tries
to identify and match the timbers used when restoring
old horses. They report that the Victorian enthusiasm
for the American timbers exported as 'pitch pine' was
not reflected in the rocking horses because it made
them too heavy. Pitch pine is a collective noun for
such trees as Pinus palustris, Pinus echinata and
Pinus Elliotti. The workshop did have one American
timber come in, which was identified as Eastern White
Pine (Pinus strobus), known in England as the Weymouth
Pine, after Lord Weymouth who introduced it in 1705.
The French call it Pin de Lord after him also. This
was a tree that grew to heights that astonished early
explorers and so its prime use by sea-faring nations
such as Britain and Portugal was for ship masts. It is
known to have reached 80m in America but the tallest
in Britain at present is only a little over half that.
Apart from timber it has been of enormous medical value
to both the native Americans and the colonists. It was,
however, as a timber tree that it came to Britain and
its culture encouraged in the 18th century. Sadly this
elegant tree proved uneconomic as it's prone to Blister
Rust which kills it. Few old trees survive but it is
still planted sometimes as an ornamental. The timber,
however, is still imported because it is so lightweight.

Apart from these hobby horses and rocking horses
there were little wooden models on wheels designed to
be pulled along on a piece of string. Larger ones were
provided with a looped handle at the back by which the
beast could be pushed along. They became popular, from
the 18th century onwards, as a way of helping a child
learn to walk. English versions were part of what
became known as 'Bristol Toys' and still exist today.
Now come in a range of designs other than just horses,
such as the very popular trolley for play bricks.

Before modern factory produce predominated, the toys
were simple items made usually of wood by dad or one
of the village craftsmen if he did not charge much.
They produced some beautiful pieces of work. Hoops
became very popular for both boys and girls and the
earlier wooden ones came from the hoopers who mass
produced them in the copses for the packaging industry.
One or two were needed in the dairy, to hold pails
apart when being lifted on a yoke. Ash and Hazel were
the chief trees for hoops. It was the wood-turner who
provided the spinning tops, as a by-product after
making a nest of bowls; the top was fashioned from the
core of the innermost bowl. Today pole-lathe workers
make rattles to demonstrate their skills, at craft
fairs. They comprise a set of rings trapped on a stick
which have been fashioned in a sequence from one piece
of wood. For these they prefer to use Ash because Oak
and Chestnut contain tannins that can upset the child
if the rattle is sucked. In the past the type of timber
mattered little, so long as it would shape well. If it
took paint and did not splinter easily so much the
better. Thus for toys in general Birch and Alder were
much used.

A turner somewhere,
perhaps in East Anglia,
made these wooden soldiers.
He turned three soldiers
end to end as one baluster,
before separating them and
then splitting each down
the middle to make the total
of six, which he then fixed
on a wooden base. They are
painted boldly in British
uniforms and a different
set for the enemy.

"King Charles II" proclaims the name plate on the side of this wooden locomotive which has 1896 on the boiler. It's all of wood, except the axles, and the wheels turn, so this could be pushed along the floor and is big enough for a small toddler to sit astride and propel along with his feet. It's painted in black and red and gold.

Both soldiers and locomotive
recorded through the courtesy
of the proprietors of the
'Antique Teapot', Ripley, Surrey.

The woodturner has split the baluster
to make pairs of flat-backed soldiers.

The enemy soldiers

BY ROYAL DECREE

Despite being so small, the British Isles have amassed an astonishing calendar of special occasions. Many are no longer practised but in going out of use it has so often been the children who have perpetuated some of the customs and rituals long after the adults have ceased to do so. It was once law that everyone must celebrate November 5th and so it remained until last century. After the law was repealed children continued to "Remember, remember, the 5th of November". With the help of the media, the reason is getting twisted. It is now popularly believed that the celebrations are because Guy Fawkes tried to blow up parliament whereas in fact we are supposed to be celebrating his failure; that King James I survived and Protestantism with him and that terrorism did not prevail.

Similarly, King Charles II had decreed that May 29th should be kept as a public holiday to celebrate his restoration to the throne. It was on this date in 1660, his thirtieth birthday, that he made his triumphant entry into London, having been proclaimed king by parliament on May 8th. He had succeeded to the throne before - on January 30th 1649 when his father, Charles I, was executed but a few days later the 'Rump' Parliament abolished the monarchy.

Thus Restoration Day came into the calendar. It also came to be known as Royal Oak Day, Oak Apple Day or Oak Ball Day in commemoration of the king evading his enemies after the Battle of Worcester (1651) by hiding in an Oak tree at Boscobel. In commemoration of this it became the custom to wear a sprig of Oak and people remember in particular the pride with which it was worn to church whenever the date fell on a Sunday. Initially it must have been a safety measure as it was so dangerous to be anything but Royalist. Many a pub changed its name to The Royal Oak rather than risk being thought a meeting place of republicans or of Catholic rebels and today the name is well-established.

Best of all was to sport a sprig
of oak bearing the growth (gall)
known as an oak apple or oak ball.
Many people think an oak apple is
the hard wooden 'marble' to be found
growing on the twigs, whereas the
wildlife books say this is the Oak
Marble Gall and that the Oak Apple
Gall is larger and softer, coloured
green and red, and growing on the
leaves. Well, as far as the celebration
is concerned the former is correct, since
the latter is caused by a gall wasp that was not
introduced into this country until about 1830.

marble
galls.

May 29th was also abolished as a public holiday last
century but some communities have continued their
traditions, such as St.Neots in Cornwall and
Castleton in Derbyshire. The parish church
became the focal point for decoration,
especially in this case since James
and succeeding monarchs have been
the Head of the Church of England,
but the houses were decked too and
even horses bore oak sprays, while
a correspondent, whose father was a
train driver, remembered that steam
locomotives were duly decked too.

Oak Apple Gall

71

Children invented their own rituals. Any who failed
to sport their oak had their feet stamped on, or were
thrashed with Stinging Nettles or pushed into a nettle
patch, hence local names such as Nettle Day in some
places. George Sturt, writing of the 1860s in Surrey
did "remember dimly an angry time when somebody's
crumpled oak-leaf was suspected of being maple"
which would indeed have caused anger; children
are very strict about following the precise
rules of their games and rituals.
However, in some localities it was
apparently acceptable to substitute
maple if oak was not available.
For the thrill of taking risks
some children would hide their
oak from sight, waiting to be
challenged and would then
produce it triumphantly at
the very last moment and
save themselves from painful
punishment.

Field Maple

   The strict rules
decreed that all must
cease at noon but how this
time for the truce was introduced
is not known. It is common to other
childhood rituals, such as practical
joking on April Fool's Day. It is possibly
Celtic, from when time was measured in nights rather
than days and therefore the turning point would be noon
rather than midnight; however, the only accepted relic
of that is our term 'fortnight' from fourteen nights.

   Local variations included differentiating between the
sexes, as in this letter from Mrs P. Turvil in 1992:-

   "In the village school which I attended in South
Staffordshire during the 1930s we never failed to
observe May 29th as 'Oak Apple Day'. It was incumbent
upon all GIRLS to wear a spray of oak. The spray HAD to
contain an oak apple. Acorns were not acceptable. Any
girl failing to wear the oak apple was beaten on the

bare legs by BOYS with bunches of stinging nettles. As, by that time of the year, long black woollen stockings had been replaced by white ankle socks this could be a very painful experience. We girls took great care to display our oak apples prominently, even going so far as to hoard them from the previous autumn in case there was none available at the correct time. For some reason that was never questioned, boys were not required to display the emblem, and no retribution was meted out to them if they failed to sport the oak apple."

Retribution on the 'traitor' included rhyming taunts such as:

> Shick-shack, shig-shag
> Put old Cromwell's head in a bag.
> Royal Oak
> The Whigs provoke.

or

> Shig-shag penny a rag
> Bury his head in Cromwell's bag
> All up in a bundle.

Thus local names include Shick-shag Day, Shick-shack Day or something similar. It is usually accepted that this derives from 'shit sack' and there are a number of rhymes where this is quite explicit! Although used in abuse against non-conformists in the religious sense, it was taken up again on this day against anyone suspected of having Cromwellian sympathies.

Children are also very adept at turning the events in the annual calendar into opportunities for begging, such as penny-for-the-guy before Guy Fawkes' Night. The same occurred on Shig-shag Day when roving bands of 'shig-shaggers' exacted donations. In some districts they demanded beer rather than money!

DAISY CHAINS

Ask a little child to draw a flower and the chances are extremely high that it will look like a Daisy. In the 17th century Nicholas Culpeper was able to write in his herbal, "These are so well known to almost every child, that I suppose it needless to write any description of them." Above all others the Daisy has been the prime flower of childhood and remains so, with junior school children singing at their Assemblies Jan Struther's words:-

"Daisies are our silver,
Buttercups our gold.
This is all the treasure
We can have or hold."

With this goes the ancient skill of making 'Daisy chains':- the piercing of the stalk of one Daisy so that the next can be threaded through, and so on until the chain is long enough to have its ends joined to form a circle. If short then it can be worn as a crown and if longer then it can be a garland. This may seem a 'childish' past-time today but has been more significant in the past.

Floral garlands are common to many of the world's cultures and sanctified into their religious services. In medieval Britain the Catholic church sanctified the use of garlands of Roses and Sweet Woodruff (Galium odoratum) on occasions such as St.Barnabas's Day (June 11th) and Corpus Christi (the Thursday after Trinity Sunday which is the first Sunday after Whit Sunday). These were banned at the Reformation. The extent to which flowers were used officially is difficult to estimate; some church records simply show payments for flowers and greenery as 'garnishing' without specifying what exactly was bought. Daisies seem to have been treated with caution, despite being the emblem of St.Margaret, as these still had pagan connections.

Nevertheless there is a legend that St.Augustine, having introduced Christianity at Canterbury, was in the habit of taking meditational walks out in the countryside where he met the local children making daisy chains. He then used the daisy to teach the children the notion that just as the shining petals were gathered around the golden heart of the flower so the souls of good Christians would be gathered around God the Father in Heaven. Similarly, legend has Augustine teaching children that the golden centre was like the sun of righteousness which would shine out, like the white petals, on all good Christian souls. These would ultimately be gathered together in Heaven just as daisies gather together in the grass. To add to this legend is a Christian myth to explain to children the origin of the red tips to the petals:- they were marked by the infant Jesus when he kissed the daisies brought as a gift to the stable by one of the shepherds who was too poor to afford any other gift.

Daisies were 'pagan' because they were associated with the faeries and the wearing of daisy chains by both boys and girls was said to prevent children being snatched by the Little Folk. Apparently this was a particular concern regarding girls immediately prior to their maturity. This may sound odd, to say the least, but it does connect with other known beliefs, such as evil spirits being afraid to pass through a circle -

hence the importance of joining the ends of the daisy chain. The one day in particular when Daisies were called upon for faerie protection was the pagan festival known to us as May Day.

A new 'daisy day' evolved this century with the founding of Empire Day in 1903 (changed to Commonwealth Day in 1957). Children took to wearing daisies in their buttonholes on their way to school, something that is remembered very widely. Even city schools got their Daisies, as in this memory of "the heart of London" received in 1985 from Mrs A. Brench:-

"We had bunches of ordinary little wild daisies (the kind that grows on lawns) sent us from somewhere in the country. The daisies were supposed to represent the Empire - the yellow centre was Britain, the heart of the Empire and the numerous petals, the colonies under its ruler."

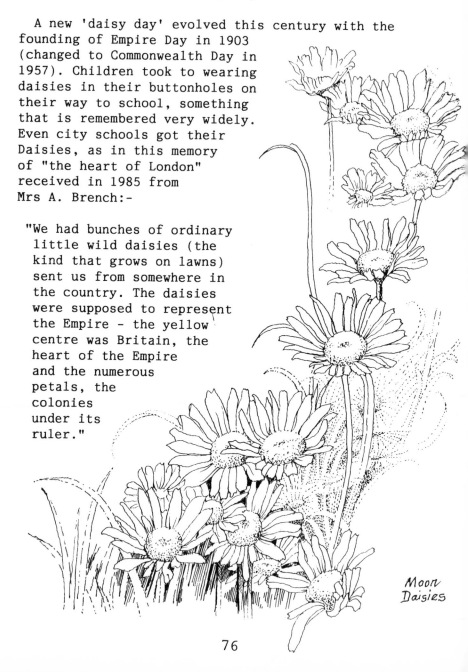

Moon Daisies

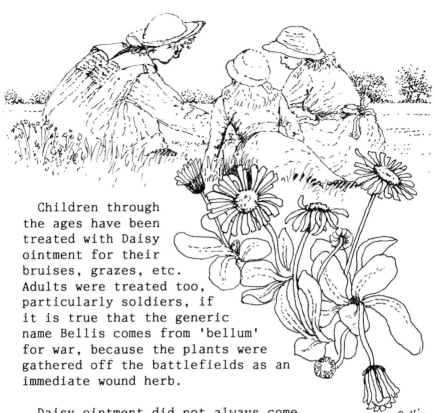

Children through
the ages have been
treated with Daisy
ointment for their
bruises, grazes, etc.
Adults were treated too,
particularly soldiers, if
it is true that the generic
name Bellis comes from 'bellum'
for war, because the plants were
gathered off the battlefields as an
immediate wound herb.

Bellis

Daisy ointment did not always come
from this plant. Also used was the larger
daisy known commonly as the Ox-eye, Moon or Dog Daisy
(Leucanthemum vulgare). Between them they have served
in the treatment of over thirty conditions. Basically
'big boys' got the larger daisy and 'little boys' got
the little one, Bellis perrenis.

It was at the height of popularity during the 14th
century and a strange piece of lore has been sent in
several times but so far the original source has not
been traced, namely, that in the Middle Ages small
was beautiful and so children were greased with daisy
ointment to stunt their growth. This was founded
on the belief that the little Daisies did not have
whatever caused the Moon Daisies to grow larger.
Don't let this make you fearful of Daisies though,
for Bellis does not contain any growth retarders.

77

"HERE WE GO ROUND THE MULBERRY BUSH"

Much has been debated about the origins of this nursery rhyme. Frequently attention has been focused upon the Mulberry in question being either the White or Black Mulberry of the genus Morus. English names are rarely so specific. The name Mulberry has been given to a wide range of plants from the Whitebeam tree to the tiny strands of the parasite Dodder. It is the Blackberry (Rubus fruticosus agg.) that has been a Mulberry in counties such as Suffolk. Once the Morus spp. were introduced into this country and grown for fruit and the juice used for colouring food and wine it's easy to see that the Blackberry could become the 'poor man's Mulberry'.

As for the nursery rhyme, that has been explained as surviving from the practice of harvesting the long new growths of the Bramble for use as binding material once the bark and thorns have been stripped off, and, that this was a winter activity for the "cold and frosty morning" of the rhyme. I remember the Brambles being so gathered in Surrey but it was not specific to the winter except in that it was at that time that the woodlands were worked and there arose the need to a strong binder to tie up the bundles of brushwood to take back as firewood. The same activity recurred in the spring when Hazel trash was cut for pea sticks, or ricers as they were then called.

The art of stripping the bark and thorns off was as simple as most traditional expedients. Two nails were driven into a nearby fence post or stump, side by side, with just enough gap to take a Blackberry stem. Then the stem was ripped through with a hard yank, in reverse direction to that in which it grew, so that then the backward pointing thorns hooked into the nails and ripped off. Simple, when you know how!

Certainly there wasn't any dancing around chanting rhymes. That would appear to be derived from a ritual rather than an everyday working practice. Arched stems of brambles that descended to the ground and took root were 'magical'; we were told as children not to crawl through them. There are records of such plant loops being used for healing and in particular for healing "ruptures" in children. From the 17th century there's John Evelyn's description in his "Silva" relating to Ash (Fraxinus excelsior):-

> "I have heard it affirmed with great Confidence, and upon Experience, that the rupture to which many Children are obnoxious, is healed, by passing the Infant through a wide Cleft made in the Bole or Stem of a growing Ash-tree, through which the Child is made to pass, and then carried a second Time round the Ash, caused to repass the same Aperture again, that the cleft of the tree suffered to close and coalesce, as it will, the Rupture of the Child, being carefully bound up, will not only abate, but be perfectly cured." (Book I, Chapter VII)

Evelyn obviously had his doubts and regularly used such expressions as "I have heard it affirmed" or "I do but report it." He needed to be 'scientific' as the book was for his fellow members at the Royal Society. This was the 17th century age of witch hunts so he certainly did not want to look at all susceptible to the 'superstitions' of the time. It was dangerous to deviate from the accepted Word of God. Other writers have confirmed this Bramble usage. It sounds ancient and in common with other calls upon the supernatural could well have been accompanied by chants, devolving as nursery rhymes like
'Here we go Round the Mulberry Bush'.

It is not the Bramble as such that is important in this ritual so much as the loop it creates. The nature of a circle or a ring has been revered for thousands of years, as symbols of eternity, as sources of great power, and so forth. As little children we were forbidden to crawl through the bramble loops arching out into the orchard grass because "You'll be taken by the Little People."

As for the Ash tree ritual that Evelyn and others have noted, that was shown to television viewers by Dr. Desmond Morris in the 1990s, being performed today in N. Italy. It was not for ruptures this time but as an initiation into manhood at puberty. The boy in the film was stripped naked and passed through a sapling that had been split and held apart. Afterwards the tree was bound together again and as it healed and grew strong so the boy would heal his childhood weaknesses and grow strongly into manhood. Worldwide there are many initiations where the mother hands over the care of the child to the man during adolescence.

Returning to the Blackberry, the ritual of passing through an arched stem rooted in the ground was used on cows. Within the last hundred years the Sussex stockmen were still dragging their sick cows through such loops. Even to the experienced stockmen it must have been quite a job, throwing a cow to the ground, shackling her and then dragging the weight through the arch, which gives some idea of the depth of belief or the desperate measures still being resorted to for something as valuable as a good milker.

The trouble with such fascinating reports is that the writer doesn't go back to assess the success rate! We could guess that a change took place on enough occasions to encourage repetition of the act, but, today we might question the cause of the change.

PENNY
A BUNCH

By dawn cities like London were well astir and so through early morning streets the flower-girls made their way to the flower markets. There they bought small bunches of flowers, preferably scented ones, which they then tried to sell on at a profit.

This became an important trade because anyone who could afford a few pennies liked to carry the scented posies to ward off the evil smells of the city. London stank, even by the standards of past ages. By late Norman times the burning of sea-coal was causing air pollution and coming under legislative restriction, then there was the poor sanitation causing not only the streets to stink but the Thames and all its side creeks and ditches and streams. Additionally there was the stench from all the industrial processes, such as tanning, dyeing to brewing, upon which London thrived and became important. By the mid 18th century it had eclipsed Paris as the most important city in Europe.

The connection between bad smells and disease was well-known long before germs were discovered. Judges carried posies to ward off 'jail fever' being brought into court by the prisoners and on three of the City's ceremonial occasions the judges still carry the posies in procession. The insect repellent Rue was much used for this.

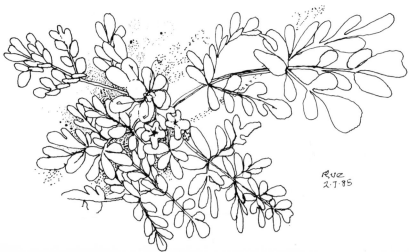

Rue
2.7.85

Her Majesty the Queen still has a warrant holder for making the royal posies but these have become symbolic and are used only for the Royal Maundy Service. The Primrose features handsomely in these.

Lesser folk relied upon the flower-girls although this trade was of course seasonal. Fortunately for the girls some of the most beautiful flowers were also scented and came in a glorious rush of spring when they must have been so very welcome after the long days of winter smogs in London. Customers were just as shrewd over prices in former times as they can be today and so it was not easy for the girls to create a profit margin over their competitors without destroying the trade. The solution was to buy bunches in multiples of three and then rebunch them into four and sell them on for the same price. Thus the slightly smaller bunch was not so noticeable and a small profit was made; just a penny in this way, last century.

Country people have always brought the flowers into the city but there were other sources. The greatest families of the realm had London houses with gardens but when the household was in the country any London surplus was sold off. The chief

market for this was in St.Paul's churchyard but the noise was a disturbance to the Cathedral services and so the market was forced out to the garden wall of the Blackfriars. Then in the 17th century market gardening developed more on the city fringes, especially when Protestant immigrants, arrived. These were primarily Huguenots, after the Massacre of St.Bartholomew and the Edict of Nantes. These people were both expert growers and great flower lovers. The market gardeners helped to popularise and develop such

Cheiranthus
species.

favourites as the Polyanthus, that became one of the select 'florist' flowers. The Wallflower was grown for market too. This was an ancient choice - the Persians grew beds of it in their paradise gardens but its generic name Cheiranthus is thought by some to come from the Greek: 'kheir' for hand, plus 'anthos' for flower, being the one carried in the hand. Its rich scent has always ensured its appeal from ancient times into the Middle Ages when it was carried at the spring fairs etc. and so on to the streets as places became urbanised. By the early 17th century growers were breeding the large-flowered strains still popular today.

One of the flower markets was to become pre-eminent and that was Covent Garden. Originally it was Convent Garden because of its connection with the Convent of St. Peter at Westminster, today's Westminster Abbey.

Apart from seasonal restrictions on the girls' livelihood there was a ban on Sunday trading. This was lifted in 1588 by Henry VIII. There were some restrictions however, such as trading having to finish by 7a.m. in the summer and 8a.m. in the winter and that each crier was restricted to no more than three baskets. The latter was aimed at other more bulky perishable goods than the tray of flowers that the girls could afford.
(source: Museum of London)

Polyanthus

84

The demand for the country flowers in the cities was not entirely as deodorants but also for sentimental reasons. As the housing and working conditions worsened in the industrial centres so there grew increasingly a nostalgic longing for the former rural days, mainly from those who had never known the countryside. They developed the idea into a sort of lost Golden Age. The Romantic movement worked with this for the literate classes, so Wordsworth's 'golden daffodils' did no harm to the flower trade any more than did the highly detailed painting of 'The Hireling Shepherd' by William Holman Hunt, with its floral detail in the foreground. At the same time, the summer of 1851, John Everett Millais was with Hunt beside the River Hogsmill at Ewell in Surrey, painting 'Ophelia' with its glorious overhang of Dog Roses. The sites have gone under suburbia, even their lodging house has gone, making the scenes as remote to us today as they would have been to the labouring classes of the cities dreaming of their lost Golden Age.

To satisfy this longing for better times and places the countryside was being stripped of its wild flowers and ferns, not just by children but the adults worked at it too. In particular the sellers wanted flowers that would withstand picking without immediately shedding their petals or wilting miserably. Thus by 1876 the Chequered Lily (Fritillaria meleagris) was exterminated in Surrey and two years later Pasque Flower (Pulsatilla vulgaris) was last recorded. The Wild Daffodil in Surrey is reduced primarily to one last site, now a reserve. The same tales can be told from many a county subject to depredations from urban centres. The expanding railway network through the 19th century hastened the decline with its rapid links between remoter areas and Covent Garden.

As late as the 1930s The Great Western Railway was
organising Daffodil Specials to the Dymock and Newent
districts of Gloucestershire where daffodils grew in
great golden swathes. Hundreds of bunches were picked
and taken to London. There was a plea at the stations
to buy a bunch for London hospitals and the railway
company transported them to the capital where the taxi
drivers joined the good-will gesture and delivered
them to the hospitals. Daffodils still flourish in the
region, with special waymarked daffodil walks between
the parishes, but the acreage
is much reduced from the
golden glory of earlier years.

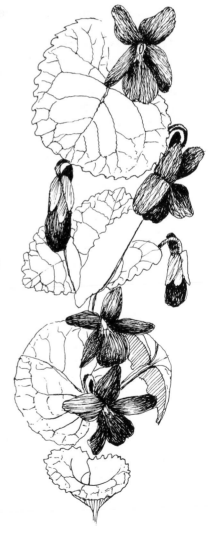

Special occasions led to
specific flower gatherings,
such as the bunches of violets
given to mothers by their
children on Mothering Sunday.
Violets came to symbolise
remembrance and if white
ones could be in the bunch so
much the better as these
symbolised loving thoughts;
all very important to children
who had left the family home -
boys to learn a trade or craft
from a distant master and girls
in domestic service. By the
First World War there were one
and a half million girls in
domestic service.

Violets were much favoured
by the girls while the boys
gave a little present of less
precise identity. Two other
options became traditional
on this day. One was a present
of a simnel cake, perhaps made
by the cook for the girls in
service. It was a rich currant
cake made with wheat flour,

taking its name probably from the Latin 'simila' for fine flour. The other special was a dish of frumenty or furmenty made from whole wheat boiled in milk and seasoned with sugar and cinnamon; this is inexpensive and easy dish to try today from a packet of crushed wheat flakes soaked in milk and cooked into firm cake.

Such presents of food were much appreciated in the poor homes, especially as the time arrives during the Lenten fast. The Church relaxed the fasting discipline for the feast days of Easter and originally Mothering Sunday was a Christian event. It derives from times when people were encouraged to visit the church of their baptism although it included parishes visiting the Cathedral of their diocese. For most people though this was a parish event, calling for a return to the home village and therefore a chance to visit mothers. The Biblical foundation for this is Galatians 4:26 which became the traditional epistle of the day,
"But Jerusalem which is above is free,
which is the mother of us all."

With the relaxing of the Lenten fast this has been known as Refreshment Sunday and is used to commemorate the parable of the Feeding of the Five Thousand and that became the gospel of the day. From the opening words of the introit 'Rejoice ye with Jerusalem' (Isaiah 66:10) derives the other name of SS Lataetere Sunday.

Nowadays Mothering Sunday is the 7th Sunday leading up to Easter, or, if it's easier, the third Sunday before Easter Day, and is known officially as Lent 4. It went into decline, especially as families broke up on such a large scale this century. It was forgotten altogether in some places, such as America, and there we find it being invented afresh by Miss Anna Jarvis, as Mothers' Day, in 1906. It stayed there until the Second World War when American Servicemen introduced it to this country and we've had Mothers' Day ever since. In England Mothers' Day is celebrated in conjunction with Mothering Sunday but in the United States the date is fixed to the second Sunday in May.

SAFFRON AND MEASLES

Finally, to the healing plants of childhood. The list seems endless. It is in fact enough to fill such famous herbals as those of John Gerard and Nicholas Culpeper, since so few plants are listed specially for healing children who were thus treated as young adults. What was good for one was good for the other. Rarely are the recommended doses reduced for children, making many recipes potentially lethal. They had the right plant but the wrong dosage, which no doubt helped contribute to the high infant mortality rates.

One such toxic plant was the Columbine. In the Middle Ages it was highly valued and used with little discrimination for almost everything. It continued against measels and smallpox until 18thC. Then the Swedish botanist Linnaeus voiced his concerns that this plant, used as a vegetable as well as a medicine, was poisonous. Children were dying from overdoses. It still took a long time before it lost its recognition as an official medicine. It ended up as poison in rat bait!

Herbal medicines were normally a mixture and Columbine was often combined with saffron, which was another cure for measles and smallpox. Saffron is an unusual plant material. It is made by baking the sex organs of the autumn flowering Saffron Crocus which itself is unusual for being sterile. It has to be reproduced vegetatively which helps explain why saffron has always been very expensive. The high cost is due to the tiny return from each plant: it takes some 4,320 flowers to yield a mere ounce of saffron. Needless to say there has always been the risk of adulterated saffron coming on to the market.

In Britain we tried adding the stigmas of spring-flowering Crocus species and even the dried petals of the Pot Marigold. These adulterants satisfy the same needs but are much inferior. Our saffron on the other hand was claimed to be the best in the world - but a good salesman would say that wouldn't he!

Columbine

Saffron Crocus; background fragment of Waverley Abbey,
Surrey, where there was a saffron ground.

One of its traditional uses came to public attention in East London in 1921 during inquests held after an outbreak of measles. The coroner for Poplar heard that the children had been treated with saffron tea, of which he was somewhat suspicious. He needn't have been. K'Eogh's Irish Herbal of 1735 said "It is very good for fevers, smallpox, and measles." In the previous century Culpeper assured readers, "It is excellent in epidemical diseases, such as pestilence, smallpox and measles," while under his entry for the adulterating Pot Marigolds he observed they are only "a little less effectual in the small-pox and measles than saffron." Before that, Gerard said, "The eyes being anointed with the same dissolved in milke or fennel or rose water, are preserved from being hurt by the small pox or measles." And so on.

The saffron treatment is ancient but the healing compounds therein are in very small amounts so it is only listed in five European Pharmacopeias (not in Britain's, which records reports of poisoning from saffron, but it is used in homeopathic medicine). The Pot Marigold or Calendula is included in thirty six preparations listed in the 1993 British Phatmacopoeia.

Hopefully by now the book should have made clear what a strange mixture of fact and faith and folklore made up everyday life. In the world of medicine that is still true today, if viewed broadly to take into account everything from spiritual faith healing to synthetic chemical drugs. What intrigues many people is how often the so-called old wives tales are being proven valid, with such lucrative revivals as using Feverfew and Evening Primrose. Even the astrology of Culpeper that has been scorned for over three hundred years is now proving of interest as the pharmaceutical companies find that it does make a difference exactly when their plants are harvested.

Happily ancient medicinal plant uses are well documented whereas many of the other uses of plants need recording fast, before they are lost for ever.

REFERENCES CITED IN THE TEXT

Culpeper, Nicholas. The English Physician, 1652.

Erichsen-Brown, Charlotte. Medicinal and Other Uses of North American Plants. Dover Pub. New York. 1979

Evelyn, John. Silva or a Discourse of Forest Trees. 5th Ed. 1759 used.

Gerard, John. The Herball, or Generall Historie of Plants. London. 1597

Gies, Frances; The Knight in History; Hale; 1984.

Godwin, Harry. The History of the British Flora. CUP, Cambridge. 2nd Ed. 1975

Harvey, John - Early Nurserymen
    Phillimore, Chichester;   1974
- Medieval Gardens, Batsford; 1981

Humphries, Steve et al. A Century of Childhood. Sidgwick & Jackson. 1988

Kelly, James, A Complete Collection Of Scotish Proverbs Explained and Made Intelligible to the English Reader. 1721.

K'Eogh, John, Botanologia Universalis Hibernica, Cork, 1735

Lewington, Anna. Plants for People. Natural History Museum. 1990

Martindale - The Extra Pharmacopoeia (Ed. James Reynolds). 30th Ed. The Pharmaceutical Press. 1993

Mills, Simon. A Dictionary of Modern Herbalism. USA. 1989

Room, Adrian. True Etymologies. Routledge. 1986

Stowe, John, The Chronicles of England. 1603

Sturt, George. Small Boy in the Sixties. CUP. 1932

Turner, William, THe Seconde Parte of William Turners Herball. 1562

Youings, Joyce. Sixteen-Century England. Penguin. 1984

CROSS REFERENCE FOR BOTANICAL NAMES

Acer campestre - Maple
Aesculus hippocastanum - Horse Chestnut
Alnus glutinosa - Alder
Althaea officinalis - Marsh Mallow
Anethum graveolens - Dill
Anthriscus sylvestris - Cow Parsley
Aquilegia vulgaris - Columbine
Arctium lappa - Burdock
Bellis perennis - Daisy
Beta vulgaris subsp. vulgaris - Sugar Beet
Betula pubescens / B.pendula - Birch
Brassica cvs - Cabbage
Calendula officinalis - Pot Marigold
Castanea sativa - Sweet Chestnut
Cheiranthus cheiri - Wallflower
Conium maculatum - Hemlock
Convolvulus arvensis - Bindweed
Cornus sanguinea - Dogwood
Corylus avellana - Hazel
Crataegus monogyna / laevigata - Hawthorn
Crocus sativus - Saffron Crocus
Euonymus europeaus - Spindle Tree
Fagus sylvatica - Beech
Foeniculum vulgare - Fennel
Fraxinus excelsior - Ash
Fritillaria meleagris - Chequered Lily
Galium odoratum - Sweet Woodruff
Galium verum - Lady's Bedstraw
Glycerrhiza glabra - Liquorice
Hedeoma pulegiodes - American Pennyroyal
Heracleum mantegazzianum - Giant Hogweed
Humulus lupulus - Hop
Ilex aquifolium - Holly
Juncus spp. - Rushes

Linum usitatissimum - Flax
Malva sylvestris - Mallow, Common
Mentha x piperita - Peppermint
 - pulegium - Pennyroyal
Morus spp. - Mulberry
Myrrhis odorata - Sweet Cicely
Paeonia spp. - Paeony
Papaver rhoeas - Poppy, Corn
Pimpinella anisum - Anise
Pinus echinata, Elliotti, palustris - Pitch Pines
 - strobus - Weymouth Pine / Eastern White Pine
Plantago lanceolata - Ribwort Plantain
Primula cvs. - Polyanthus
Pteridium aquilinum - Bracken
Pulsatilla vulgaris - Pasque Flower
Quercus robur / petraea - Oak
Ranunculus (yellow spp.) - Buttercups
Rosa spp & cvs. - Roses
Rubus fruticosus agg. - Blackberry / Bramble
Ruta graveolens - Rue
Saccharum officinale - Sugar Cane
Salix spp. - Willow
Sambucus nigra - Elder
Sorbus aucuparia - Rowan
Sphagnum spp. - Moss
Taraxacum officinale - Dandelion
Taxus baccata - Yew
Thymus spp. - Thyme
Typha latifolia - Reedmace
Ulmus procera agg. - Elm
Ulex europaeus
Urtica dioica - Nettles, Stinging
Viola spp. - Violets

INDEX

For a list of other
titles in this series
write to Chris Howkins,
70 Grange Road,
New Haw, Addlestone,
Surrey. KT15 3RH